Life
is not
Personal

Spiritual teachings
for daily life

Michael Kewley
Dhammachariya Paññadipa

All rights reserved.

No part of this publication may be reproduced, stored in a retrieval system or transmitted, in any form or by any means, electronic, mechanical, photocopying, recording or otherwise, without prior permission of the publishers.

This book is sold subject to the condition that it shall not by way of trade or otherwise, be lent, re-sold, hired out or otherwise circulated without the publishers prior consent in any form of binding cover other than that in which it is published and without similar condition including this condition being imposed on the subsequent purchaser.

Copyright©Michael Kewley 2009

Published by:
Panna Dipa Books.
ISBN: 978-1-899417-06-3

E-mail:
dhammateacher@hotmail.com

Life is not personal

For Isabelle

Introduction

The truth, and the way to live a beautiful and valuable life, is not a secret to be shared only amongst a few. It is something to be realised by everyone.
It is not held or hidden in a special place or guarded by a particular group of people.
It is something immediate to all of us, if we are brave enough to go beyond the limitations of culture, religion and social conditioning.
Our journey is not an outward journey to an exotic Eastern country, but a quiet beautiful voyage to the heart, the place of peace and the home of truth.

This book then, is only a series of simple reminders to re-awaken us to the truth. To remind us of that which we have forgotten.

You're not the body and you're not the mind – so who is suffering?

Whatever we attach to will hurt us.

You're not broken, you don't need to be fixed.

The greatest gift we can give ourselves and the world, is the truth. To make an effort to be free and to live a beautiful life that has value, not only for ourselves, but for all beings.

It is not my intention to give a series of 'spiritual

sounding quotations' for you to casually drop into conversations to impress your friends when you drink a coffee together, but a real and powerful reminder of reality. A direct wake up call to the heart!
With each 'quotation', I offer a short explanation, a gesture to point the way, but none of these truths can be understood or grasped through the intellect. They come from the heart, and can only be received by the heart. Don't read this book from cover to cover, but simply open it occasionally and see what it reveals.

And remember, the truth is like a joke, you either get it or you don't get it, but it cannot be explained. So be patient and allow the truth to show itself to you. There is nothing here for you to 'figure out', only something to be shared. So relax, be open and everything will be revealed.

May all beings be happy

Michael Kewley
Dhammachariya Paññadipa
Southern France
May 2009

- 1 -
No-one ever lay on their death bed and said, 'I wish I'd spent more time at work.'

Where do your priorities lie? Do you put your energy into the things you believe in, or simply follow the same old routine? However otherwise it may seem, no-one is making you do anything. You are responsible for your life, and how you live it. So stop for a moment and reflect, 'Am I doing the things that are important to me, or am I being sidetracked by convention and fear?'

At the end of your time, who's life will you have lived, yours, or someone else's?

- 2 -
If life doesn't turn out exactly as you planned - don't be surprised.

If life doesn't turn out exactly as you planned...

*L*ife is the great unknown. Even though we plan and scheme and make millions of assumptions about the future, the truth is that we don't know what can happen in the next moment, let alone the next five weeks, months or years. So don't be surprised when things don't go according to your ideas, just relax and remember, life isn't personal, it's just life. Be open to the ever changing conditions and flow with them. Don't get stuck. The moment you feel free to respond fully and freely to life, you are already more powerful than can know.

- 3 -
You can't think your way to peace.

You can't think your way to peace.

The mind is the architect of our life, and can prove itself to be our best friend or our greatest enemy.

Of course, the mind itself is just the mind, it is how we use it that determines its value to us.

Our social and cultural conditioning is to use the mind to be busy, to wonder, plan and speculate, always believing that we can think our way to the place of peace and happiness in our life. But happiness, true and lasting happiness, is the place beyond the thinking, restless mind.

In the moment when the continual mental activity falls away, there is contentment, there is rest, there is peace. There is the wonderful 'simply being' in the moment.

Here is the happiness that is not conditioned by the external world, and the mind filled with its thoughts, desires and aversions.

So try to let go little more. Stop trying to control everyone and everything and allow things to be just as they are. When you arrive in this place, you are already in the place of peace.

- 4 -
The choices we make determine the life we live.

The choice we make determine the life we live.

So what are you choosing today, to live from love or to live from fear? The choice is yours. Love is always our strength, and fear is always our weakness.

When we follow our fear, no matter how subtle and justifiable it may be, we continually compromise ourselves in our life, and believe that what we do, we do for ourselves. Actually, we just follow the same old path – the path of our parents, the path of our education, the path of our culture and society.

We have to know for ourselves that there is no absolute and right way to live, except the way of love, compassion, joy and wisdom. It is always a big mistake to believe that there is something in the world that is worth compromising our honesty and integrity for.

Find your heart, and follow your own path. Live your life!

- 5 -

**People are the way they are, that is their choice.
You are the way you are, that is your choice!**

*E*ven though we may often feel it, we are not victims in this life. In every moment we are making choices and decisions as to how we are, and how we can be. For the most part this is not recognised and we feel directed by outward conditions. But you are in control - you just don't know it!

So, guard your energy and stop judging others, they are acting according to their fears and desires, and they will have to face the consequences of what they do. Look at yourself, where are you coming from?

Honestly and directly ask yourself, 'What is my agenda?' 'Why do I put my effort here?' 'What is it that I want?' 'Why am I doing this?'

When we are clear about our real motivations in life everything becomes simple and we cease to be the victims of someone else's, and more importantly, our own delusions.

Life is not personal

- 6 -
Perspective.

Perspective.

*P*erspective is perhaps, the most useful asset in our lives. To see and know the reality of each situation without being confused by it. When we have no real or accurate perspective we can often feel ourselves to be like a cork on the waves, being dashed first here and then there, without any real control in our lives. For our own peace of mind we need to know what is important, what is less important and what is meaningless!

When we have perspective in the moment we are able to respond to life from a position of balance, without making even the smallest thing a crisis!

Being late for an appointment is not a crisis. Missing the bus is not a crisis. Over sleeping in the morning is not a crisis. These are just things that happen, they are part of our ordinary, everyday life, and we have to keep them in perspective. Remember, everything that happens in your life only has the power and the value that you give it. The moment that we have perspective in life, we will know what needs to be done and what can be let go of. In this way, we will have real peace, real happiness and real value.

- 7 -
Whatever we attach to will hurt us.

Whatever we attach to will hurt us.

We attempt to make our life secure by accumulating and holding onto things, whether they be people, material possessions or ideas. But nothing is secure. Everything can be taken away from us in one way or another, and if they can be taken away, were they really ours in the first place?

So let go of these inevitably insecure attachments, and be with things as they are.

In this way we can enjoy all the beautiful things life can offer without grasping or wishing they would stay forever, and endure the difficult things that still come to us without needless suffering.

This is the beauty of wisdom. To recognise, accept and harmonise with the truth. Now we can flow with life and be happy.

- 8 -
Life is just a game.

Life is just a game.

*H*ow many times each day do we forget this? Life is a game, sometimes complicated, sometimes simple, but always the same.

And games are meant to be played, to be enjoyed, to stretch us so we can find and use our potential to bring us into our life. The idea of winning and losing is what changes a game from a personal challenge of skill, joy and integrity into a battle aimed only at defeating the other. The moment we choose success and victory over failure and defeat, we loose our balance and so loose the pleasure of playing. In that very moment we become the victim to our own desires.

Look how we view sport. When we simply watch a competition between two players or teams we can enjoy the individual skill of the protagonists. The moment we choose one side over another, the doors to our unhappiness and frustration fly open.

Therefore, the wise person lets go of choosing victory over defeat, success over failure and takes pleasure in playing the game. Winning and loosing are short term goals held by short sighted people. In the end only that which brings real and lasting happiness into our life has value.

- 9 -
**Whatever you think you are,
you are not.**

Whatever you think you are, you are not.

We formulate an identity from what we do rather than who we are. We become stuck in an idea created from conditioning. But in truth, there is nothing that we really are, and no way we have to be. These are just ideas. When we look behind these ideas we will see they are empty. The mind is moving in every moment and we cannot fix it to a time or place or idea. Whatever we grasp at as our identity, is just a movement of the mind and as soon as it has arisen, it has passed.

So stop clinging to the mind and reflect; when you are alone in the house, what are you?

Are you a mother or a father, an office worker, a bus driver? And when you wash the dishes is a dish washer really what you are? These are transient identities appropriate to time, place and circumstance, but none of them are you!

Remember, freedom is not something to get, it is something to realise. You are already free and the only limitations you face in your life are the ones that you impose upon yourself.

- 10 -
No-one's indispensable!

*F*rom our insecurities we make our life and what we do important. We create the delusion that without us, the world, or at least the small world of our family, friends and work, will stop. But it is a delusion! The reality is that no matter who we are and no matter what we do, the world will continue without us. We just won't be there to organise it, that's all! If the Prime Minister of England dies tonight, the government will continue, the country will continue, life will continue. Even the death of the most important political figure in the country will not change our day-to-day life. If the Dalai Lama dies tonight the tradition of Tibetan Buddhism will continue.

Life continued, even after the Beatles.

The realisation that we are not indispensable is a turning point in our spiritual life. To know from the heart, our own true value. Knowing that we are not indispensable, we will begin to take care of ourselves and not be the victims of the personal whims of friends, family and work. Making the time to relax and enjoy ourselves. Valuing our own life, and our own pleasures.

Serving and helping others is a beautiful activity, the real heart of spiritual understanding, but only when we act from the knowledge that is not always necessary for us to be the ones to do it.

- 11 -

**The world that we experience
is the one that we create for ourselves,
moment after moment.**

The world that we experience is the one...

We grasp at the mind and its endless mental projections believing that what we experience is what we are, but in reality, we are always the experiencer, not the experience. Everything in our mind arises and passes away, but what we empower becomes our reality. Learn to take one step back from the workings of the mind and taste the reality. You are not your mind, so don't get caught up in things that by their very nature are already moving away.

When we empower suffering and unhappiness, our world becomes a world of suffering and unhappiness. When we empower balance and peacefulness, balance and peacefulness becomes our reality. Even though we can often feel like a ball in a pin ball machine, being bounced violently from many different things beyond our control, truly the quality of our experience of life comes from our mind and our relationship to it.

Remember, how you experience this moment is personal and is dependent only on you, so empower something beautiful, something worthy, something joyful!

- 12 -
It is not my responsibility to make you happy.

It is not my responsibility to make you happy.

*I*t is common in relationships for one person to take on the role of making the other person happy. Big mistake!

Happiness is always unique and personal, and what made someone happy one time cannot be guaranteed to be successful another.

Your happiness comes from you, someone else's happiness comes from them. It cannot be given, taken away, or even shared. Look at your own life. Look to be happy yourself, because when you're happy you will be lighter and more open. You will flow with the ever changing conditions of life without complaining or making a fuss. Now you can really contribute to all your relationships with everyone with everything.

- 13 -
Let life come to you.

Let life come to you.

*I*t is said that 'patience is a virtue', but in our ordinary, everyday life we can often feel very, very far from this particular quality. It seems that the clock is always ticking and that time is rarely on our side. Everything is needed now, or sooner, and we are always behind.

As a consequence to the external pressures we meet in life, we loose our balance and so loose the sense of patience, the ability to allow things to take their own time.

Our food is forced with chemicals and steroids so we can have it earlier than its natural time, our children develop adult bodies and mentalities earlier than necessary and so miss the joy of childhood, and to wait five seconds for the internet to send or receive a message now, is almost intolerable!

When we live from this position it is easy to miss what life truly offers. To be fixated on a particular idea or thing alone means that we loose our peripheral vision of life and so don't see other possibilities. Because of this there can be so many beautiful opportunities missed.

Ambition is not the quality to empower, but clarity is!

Know what you want, know what you don't want and patiently, lovingly and gently put your energy in that direction. Make the space in your day to let life come to you.

- 14 -
Everything you want – you already have.

Everything you want - you already have.

We spend so much time and energy trying to get things from outside to make us happy, that we forget what is truly valuable. Often, if we reflect honestly, our whole spiritual journey can be seen as the continuing habit of mind to make the external world and all it contains always perfect for us. Often we feel that there are so many things about our life that we need to change people and relationships, work and social situations, finance and leisure time, but in reality there is only one thing we ever need to change – the fearful part of us that obscures our real heart.

When that has changed, everything has changed. This heart does not need to be created or achieved. It is already perfect and just waiting for you.

When the Buddha realised his enlightenment under the Bodhi tree in India two thousand six hundred years ago, he smiled.

The same smile waits for you the moment you reconnect with the love and joy in your heart. Everything beautiful and worthy that you have always wanted is there, gift wrapped and ready to open. Don't delay, a new life is waiting!

- 15 -
I'm not the body, I'm not the mind.

I'm not the body, I'm not the mind.

*T*his is the investigation of all honest meditators. A reflection for daily life to free us from the limiting attachment to mind and body as being who and what we are. The body is constantly changing, moment to moment, day by day to the end of its life span. We cannot change it's course, and our influence on it is minimal. Birth, sickness, old age and death. This is the nature of the body.

Only when we are able to harmonize with this natural dynamic will we be able to live peacefully with it, and enjoy all the physical pleasures that can be enjoyed and patiently endure, without complaint, the more difficult things that still come our way.

The mind is a constant stream of thoughts, moods, feelings and emotions, arising and passing away without end. Some of these are pleasant and some are unpleasant, but either way, their nature is the same. To be impermanent. Nothing lasts for more than a moment, and nowhere in either of these processes can we stop and declare – this is me!

When we look for 'self' we don't find anything except a continuing process of being.

This is a serious investigation that gently takes us to peace and harmony with life as we let go of the limiting delusion of self.

If we are not the body, and we are not the mind, who is it that suffers? Who is it that feels insulted or humiliated? Who is it that gets old, gets sick and dies?

To let go of unhappiness is useful. To let go of the cause of unhappiness is that which has true value!

- 16 -
Let go of hope and be free.

Let go of hope and be free.

Hope is another trap of the mind. It is a romantic device that will always keep us prisoner. As long as we are caught in the concept of hope, we are caught in the mind of the victim.

To 'hope for the best', 'hope things will work out', 'hope nothing goes wrong', 'hope I won't get hurt this time', shows only that we let go of our personal power in life and put our trust and faith in an idea.

Of course trust is important, but what we need to trust is our own integrity and judgement. We need to be the conscious architects of our life, making our choices, making our decisions and standing by the consequences of them. Life is something to interact with, it is a game to play. Don't be on the sidelines hoping for the best, try to be clear about what you want and put your energy, in that direction.

Be awake and be clear, this way everything you want will come to you.

- 17 -

We are always someone else's fool.

We are always someone else's fool.

Look around you. Aren't people idiots? Look at what they say, look at what they do, look at how they live, look at how they drive!

Why can't everyone be more like me. Perfect, well, O.K. nearly perfect. Yes, I make a few mistakes sometimes, and sometimes I get things wrong, but actually, it's never my fault.

Sound familiar? This is how we think – all of us. We are always the fool or idiot of another, because we all continually judge one another. We look from our position of fear and conditioning, and make the demand that everyone we have any contact with at all, always think, do and say exactly what we want them to. When they can do this we can relax, we can feel safe, we can feel secure.

But until then – look out world!

We will judge, blame and condemn everyone who is different from our perception of how they should be and so struggle through our life, day by day.

Unfortunately, and as hard as this may be to believe, right now there is a good chance that someone is doing exactly that to you.

Don't worry, it's not personal – it's just another manifestation of our fear. Don't wait for the other to change, simply let go of this habit of mind, and allow everyone to be as they are. This way you will be happier and more at peace, and your life will be the blessing that, right now, you cannot even imagine.

- 18 -
Acceptance.

Acceptance.

The secret to happiness in this life, is not to mind. To be accepting of the reality of each situation in each moment. Even if we don't like it. Even if we don't approve of it. Even if we don't want it!

The reality is that which is actually happening, and we are part of it. It is the truth unfolding before our very eyes. The moment we accept and harmonise with this truth we are free from the power of fear.

So accept the reality of the moment and respond with love, respond with compassion, respond with wisdom. Don't build a fantasy life around your personal views and opinions as to how everyone and everything should be. They are not the truth, they are only the conditions for your unhappiness. So let go of this limited way of living and be one with the reality of the moment. Be happy.

- 19 -
This is this.

*L*ife is imagination. It's a movie. It's a T.V. show. The images, the ideas, the concepts that surround us are actually only fantasies. Non of them are real, and in fact all of them only ever have the power that we give them. Fear, depression, love, joy, the emotions of life seem so important, so powerful. These are the things we want, and the things we don't want, the things we like and the things that we don't like. But all of them have a life force of their own and they all come and go as they please. When happiness arises we feel good, when unhappiness arises we feel bad. They are the masters, and we are the poor helpless victims. But once again, this is just another fantasy. Fear is only fear. It is an impermanent movement of mind that comes and goes by itself, but in reality it only ever has the power and influence that we give it. Happiness is the same, it arises and passes away due to conditions, but in the end, the things we want and the things we don't want, are only fear and happiness. When we understand this, the real nature of the mind and so the real nature of life, we are free.

Our world is comprised of and conditioned by the mental states that we empower. Nothing exists outside the mind, and this mind is our world. So, see things as they are. Don't be afraid. You won't loose anything, but you will gain everything. To understand that things are only things, that this is this, is to know freedom in your life. So when something pleasant arises in your life, enjoy because it's only this and it won't last. When something unpleasant arises, relax, this too is only this and it also will pass. Don't make more of it than there really is.

- 20 -
**I know what I'm saying,
I don't know what you're hearing.**

I know what I'm saying, I don't know what you'e hearing.

The world we experience is completely unique and personal to us. It is determined only by the mind that we call 'ours', and this mind is determined by our conditioning, our personal habits, our society, our culture and most importantly, by our fear. Even though we may share a common language, our subtle understanding of each and every word will be different, because the mind and our personal influences on it, are different. So, when I say 'dog' perhaps you hear, 'warm, cuddly, friendly little animal', or perhaps you hear, 'dangerous and potentially savage animal that should never be allowed into a house'.

Do you understand?

The word is the word, but the understanding of the word is unique and personal to each one of us.

The spiritual world is exactly the same. I say 'Let go'. What do you hear? I say 'Surrender into life'. What do you hear? When I speak, I speak only of love, freedom and happiness.

What do you hear?

- 21 -
Your life is always about you.

Your life is always about you.

When you wake up in the morning your first thought of the day is you. How you feel, what you want, what you don't want. You. Everything is always about you. Reflect on this. It's important. Your life is about you. The beginning, the middle and the end. Even if you are thinking about your partner, your children, your parents, your work or your friends, it's always about you!

Whatever the thought, it comes from you, and because it comes from you, in some way, subtle or gross, it's about you. It's about your desires, it's about your fears, it's about you!

But now you need to understand something important, something crucial to your continuing spiritual development.

It's O.K. There is nothing wrong with this situation at all. It's normal. It's how things are, so don't be alarmed. You are not more selfish or conceited than the next person – you are not less either – whatever you may think.

So, know this and be free. What you do, even though you think you do it for another, in reality, you do it for yourself. You do it for the subtle feelings that this thought or action brings. No problem there, provided you are not deluding yourself, so enjoy – do it, and do it well. You are doing it for yourself anyway.

> Let go a little and there is a little peace.
> Let go a lot and there is a lot of peace.
> Let go completely – complete peace.

- 22 -
The way of Letting go.

The way of letting go.

Ah, here we have it, the perfect way to perfect peace – to a perfect life. Our life is a reflection of what we hold, of what we carry. It is our attachments that determine the quality of our life, and attachments, in the end, are only ideas. So we let go of our ideas as to how everyone and everything should be, accept and then respond to things as they are. To demand that everything in life should always be perfect for us is futile. To flow with life as it manifests in each moment is true wisdom.

So the teaching is always simple, let go, let go, let go, until there is no more to let go of. Now your suffering and discontent has ended, and happiness, real and profound happiness is here.

Letting go is always the solution to your difficulties, so try this whenever you feel any kind of unhappiness in your life, whether it is anger, fear or stress, ask yourself this question,

'In this moment, what am I holding on to?'

The answer is always an idea of how this moment should be for you to feel happy. The instant that you let go of the attachment to that thought, you are free.

So try. Take a deep breath and be honest. See if you can be bigger than your idea!

- 23 -
Only ego suffers.

Only ego suffers.

It seems that we are always busy making our life look and feel important. When we explain what we do, it is always special and different, because we are special and different. Our job descriptions change even when the work is the same. We obtain certificates and papers to say how clever, talented or intelligent we are, but actually, we are the same as everyone else. Our life is filled with meaningless tasks and duties, and because they are meaningless and we know it, we make them important, firstly to ourselves and then others. We show how we have some special skill or ability, or how we need special equipment or special training, and that no-one else can do what we do. It's what we show to the world, but it's just nonsense. It's just ego and it's just life.

Some things are easier than others, some things are more difficult than others, but in the end, it's just life. When you forget this, you suffer. You feel inadequate and so always feed the need to explain and justify what you do. So don't empower this feeling, because that's just ego, and only ego suffers. Remember that what is truly important in life is not competition or being superior and showing something special in front of others, but only sharing your beautiful self with the world. Sharing your love, compassion and joy.

Do what you do, don't explain it, don't justify it, don't try to show something special or make a point, just do it and enjoy!

- 24 -
Knowing the world.

Knowing the world.

As contradictory as it may sound, we cannot know the world through the media. The stories and reports received from the newspapers, magazines and television, are always someone's personal interpretation of the event.

Even if we pride ourselves on being impartial, impartiality is something that cannot truly exist, as the world we experience is always unique and personal to us. The perception of what we experience is always determined by our own story, our own history, our own past. We like or we don't like, according to our own personal story. We approve or we don't approve according to our own personal story. We accept or we don't accept, according to our own personal story.

Truly knowing the world can happen only when we know ourselves. When we know the reality of this mind with its thoughts, moods, feelings, emotions, with its fantasies, its ideas, with its love and with its fears. Once we realise that everything we experience through the senses and the mind, is only our own personal interpretation of the event, we will stop being deluded. We will stop living our life based solely on our personal and always limited views and opinions, and we will be free from continually judging others and the situations we find ourselves in. Now we can celebrate this life as the beautiful gift that it is.

- 25 -
Everything brought us here.

Everything brought us here.

How do you regard your life? Is it a series of mistakes and errors, or a fantastic learning opportunity? You decide, because however you feel about it, it is those very incidents that brought you to this moment now. All the good moments you had, and all the bad ones.

Remember all those parts of your life that you now judge harshly and reflect, without them where would you be, what would you understand, what teaching would you have received?

And in the end you are here. No more than that.

So, there is nothing to regret, nothing to hold on to, nothing to keep and nothing to loose. Just moment after moment, response after response, lesson after lesson.

So, after all these things and all this life, what can we know if we are wise?

Live with love, wisdom, joy and compassion.

Why? Because it's better for you!

A life established in love has real and lasting value. A life without love is like an empty cup waiting to be filled.

And remember, your journey is not yet finished. Every moment we continue to make history, our history, our story. How will you remember the next moment ?

- 26 -
We may not always know what we want, but we always know what we don't want.

We may not always know what we want...

*E*veryday we are faced with thousands of choices, some simple and mundane, others difficult and complex. That we are not always so certain of what we want is understandable, so rather than try to figure out what we want, it can be sometimes easier to look at what we don't want.

When we fully know ourselves at the heart or intuitive level of mind, the difficulty in decision making falls away as we find ourselves to be more in harmony with life and so naturally more open and receptive to it's direction.

But, until that time arrives fully, take the other view. Look at what you don't want in your life.

As an illustration of this we can decide that (for example), 'I don't want years of debt...', and so not take on the responsibilities of the new car, or house.

Perhaps we can decide that, 'I don't want to be alone in my life...', and so begin to move into the area of new personal relationships.

We don't need to always know what we want, we only need to know what we don't want. Life becomes much simpler and clear when we listen to our heart, because the heart cannot and does not lie.

So when you ask yourself, quietly and honestly, 'Do I really want this?' listen to your heart.

All the answers are there.

- 27 -

Changing your life is mostly about remembering to be different.

Changing your life is mostly about remembering to be different.

We are truly creatures of habit. We find ourselves instructed in a way of living and being, and then follow that, no matter what! Familiarity become comfortable for us, and so we hold on tight. We follow the habit of identifying with the mind and it's habits of greed, hatred and delusion, and wonder why we don't meet peace in our life. We follow our habit of arguing and fighting with others, and wonder why we always complain and meet difficulties. We follow the habit of pursuing the causes of our unhappiness, and never even realise it!

The potential for all human beings is enlightenment, complete liberation from these causes of unhappiness, but even if we want it, we often forget to make the effort required, and so return to our habits of blindly following the mind.

Everything we want is already waiting for us, always available and ready to access, we just have to remember to be different.

How is it possible for us to stop smoking? Simply don't take the next cigarette! This is how we stop.

Even though it may be difficult, we have to remember to be different from our usual way of being, from blindly following our usual course of action. To be free from our habits. To let go of greed, hatred and delusion and realise our new life. Don't forget!

- 28 -
You're not broken,
you don't need to be fixed.

You're not broken, you don't need to be fixed.

Very often we look at ourselves and our life, and don't like what we see. Somewhere in our past we have been given a model of what the successful man or woman should be, and when we don't match that, we feel a sense of failure. But why?

Our life is always filled with the ideas of other people, whether through society, religion, film or the media, but whoever these people are, unless they are enlightened, they are only as confused as everyone else. Different, but not necessarily wiser, and it is wisdom that is the key to peace and happiness in our life.

Take a moment and look in the mirror. Enjoy what you see. It's a good face and a good body. Smile at the person that looks back at you. Relax and let go of an idea of how you and your life should be.

There's nothing wrong here, except perhaps that you don't match someone else's idea of how you should be. But our strength is in wisdom, and when we are wise we will make a life that has value for us and leave stereotypes and conformity to others.

You're not broken and you don't need to be fixed, so relax, be happy and enjoy your life.

- 29 -
When we stop seeking happiness, happiness comes by itself.

When we stop seeking happiness, happiness comes by itself.

*I*t is a common mistake to believe we have to work hard for happiness, or that happiness is conditioned by what we have, and who we are in society. Happiness is the experience of mind when there is no presence of fear. That's all. It's simple.

As with everything in the truly spiritual life, that which is valuable comes only when we have relinquished that which is invaluable – when we have let go.

So don't seek happiness, let go of your fears and obsessions, let go of your doubts and worries, and look, there it is!

- 30 -
Belief is not Truth.

Belief is not Truth.

Belief is an important aspect of our life. It is what protects us from the Truth. We have to understand that we only believe in things that we do not know for ourselves to be true. Once we know it, we don't have to believe it.

Do you understand?

The very knowing of Truth is not an idea, it is not faith, it is not trust. It is not what someone told us, or something we read or heard somewhere. It is not religion.

It is Truth, based upon our own personal investigation into life, and our own intuitive understanding. The mark of the true spiritual seeker is to go past the understanding of the teacher, and realise the truth for ourselves. This cannot be done through belief – no matter how great the teacher!

Belief is not truth. Belief is what we cultivate when we don't know the truth.

So, what must we do? Wake up! Wake up to reality!

Don't believe anything, but stay centred and be open to everything!

This is how to live your own life.

- 31 -
**Whatever we experience
only has the power we give it.**

Whatever we experience only has the power we give it.

Life is full of experiences. Actually, this is not true. Life is one continuing experience, and some aspects of this experience are pleasant, and some are not. Some are joyful and some are painful, but whatever they are, their reality is that they are impermanent. Nothing lasts for more than the shortest duration of time and whatever we experience only ever has the power and influence in our lives that we give it. This is an important truth to realise! Whatever we hold on to will hurt us. Whatever we make important will cause us pain. Whatever we believe becomes our truth. But the Absolute Truth, the Dhamma, is clear; Anger is only anger, fear is only fear, doubt is only doubt. Everything is arising and passing away, and has only the power we give it.

So look at your life. Look at what you hold on to. Look at what you empower. There is nothing worth fighting for, nothing worth killing for, and nothing worth dying for. There are only ideas. There are only movements of mind, and each one is only what it is, until you take hold of it and make it into your own personal world!

- 32 -
I am not responsible for how you feel.

I am not responsible for how you feel.

*T*he world you live in is unique and personal to you, and whatever feelings you have in this world come only from you. All the good ones, and all the bad ones. This is the great secret of life. No-one is doing this to you. You do it to yourself through your habit of holding on to your thoughts, ideas, views and opinions and deciding how everyone and everything in the world should be in every moment. But actually, they are just thoughts, ideas, views and opinions. They are not realities. They come from you and only ever have the power that you give them.

No-one can make you happy, except you. No-one can make you unhappy, except you.

In our life we are surrounded by millions of conditions that lead us always into one of these two extreme positions of mind. The great delusion is that the condition and the feeling is the same thing. It's not, of course, and we can know this easily if we cultivate even a little awareness in our life. Getting what you want cannot be guaranteed to bring happiness. Loosing what you have does not necessarily bring unhappiness. Without investigation it always seems different from this and we spend so much of our time and energy blaming the world and the things in the world for how we feel in this moment. But it's just an appearance. It's part of being asleep in life.

The way of freedom is to be awake in life, to see the reality of life and to celebrate this life.

- 33 -
Only love opens our heart.

Only love opens our heart.

The most powerful force in the universe is love. Even though it may not feel like this many times in a day, it is the truth. When we open our heart and realise our own unconditional love and acceptance, we become powerful figures in our own life. This life is full of possibilities. With love we are open to these possibilities. Life becomes the adventure and we take the ride. Sometimes it can be exciting, sometimes dull, but we are there, ready for change and open to all possibilities. To flow with life, and to live with and from love.

Fear closes us down to life. Fear sees danger everywhere and always tries to calculate risk and so play safe. Without understanding we miss the point. We miss the adventure that is life.

However we live, alive and with love, or afraid and with fear, we will all die.

So, live now, and live with love. This is your life. Celebrate, don't miss this moment, it is not certain there will be another one.

- 34 -

There is nothing that you really are, and no way you have to be.

There is nothing that you really are, and no way you have to be.

Conforming is always playing it safe! If we truly investigate the mystery of self, as the Buddha did, we will find the same truth he found. How can it be different. Truth is Truth. And what is this great Truth? Simple. Behind everything there is only emptiness. Everything we can know is impermanent, and only has the power or reality we give it. In truth, there is nothing that you really are. Everything that builds up your identity is illusion. It's an idea. The idea to be young or old, tall or short, fat or thin, rich or poor, man or woman, French or English, only exists when held up against its opposite.

You are only a parent in front of your children. You are only a child in front of your parent. You are only the teacher in front of the student. You are only the student in front of the teacher.

When you are alone in your home – what are you then? So, there is nothing that you really are, and so it must follow, no way you have to be. This is just more mind stuff. More social and cultural control.

What a man is, what a woman is, don't be deluded by the ideas of others. The world is occupied by unenlightened beings telling everyone how they should be.

Be true to your 'no-self' and flow in your life.

- 35 -

We only suffer when we oppose the truth.

We only suffer when we oppose the truth.

There is a little voice inside your head that sometimes shouts at you, saying, 'It shouldn't be like this!'

Don't listen. Your life must not be about what should or shouldn't be. It must be about acceptance to the moment, and then a response from the heart, whatever that response is!

Our unhappiness only arises when we don't get what we want. That's all. It's profound, and a little disturbing. Our unhappiness only arises when we don't get what we want. When we oppose what is. When we oppose the Truth.

So, if your relationship ends, accept and move on, if your career ends, accept and move on. If something you wanted to keep is lost or broken, accept and move on. This is not a platitude. It is reality.

Acceptance to the moment is the secret of happiness – even if we have to accept something we don't like – it's still happening, and that is what we have to accept!

Enjoy what you have when you have it – don't wait until it's gone!

- 36 -

**Everyone is equally important,
and everyone is equally stupid.**

Everyone is equally important, and everyone is equally stupid.

There is an old saying, 'The difference between the enlightened man and the stupid man is that the enlightened man knows'.

Enlightenment is not some special quality available to only a select few beings living in India or Tibet. It is knowing, completely, without doubt or reservation, the Truth. The Absolute Reality. That's all!

And enlightenment, the absolute knowing of Truth, is available to all, you just have to want it enough. You just have to want it more than you want anything else.

But until that moment arrives, we live in the same world as everyone else, and in that world everyone is equally important. Ideas, views and opinions are just that, ideas, views and opinions. Before enlightenment they are based in misunderstanding, of believing the unreal to be real. And so even though people may be important, and have degrees and scholarships, or hold high positions in various institutions and religions, without enlightenment, they are only as intelligent or as stupid as everyone else. Not better, not worse, just different, and equally lost! The problems with groups, committees and even governments is that they are led and directed by unenlightened beings. People may be well educated and intelligent, but as long as they are not enlightened their views and policies will not be better that anyone else's – only different!

Intelligence is not wisdom, and it is only wisdom, the beautiful manifestation of love and compassion, that will save the world from it's suffering.

- 37 -
See me!

See me!

We all want to be recognized. We all want to be seen. Standing behind our mother when we are children and she is too busy to turn around, to now, standing in our life in front of our family, friends and colleagues.

See me. See who I am. See I am someone. See I am important. See me!

This pitiful cry from the depths of our self, this aspect of our deepest suffering.

The only person who needs to see us, is ourselves. All the rest don't matter at all!

When we can see our place in our own life, we will stop looking for the acknowledgement of others. If they can't see you, it's because they are not able to see themselves. If they can't acknowledge you, it's because they are not able to acknowledge themselves. If they can't have love for you, truly, it is because they are not able to have love for themselves.

Don't wait to be seen, show your loving, beautiful self in every moment. Those who have clear eyes will see.

- 38 -
Life is not personal – it's just what happens.

Life is not personal - ist's just what happens.

Ah, life! We talk about life as though we know what it is. We talk about 'my life', and 'my mind' and 'my body', 'my family', 'my health', 'my car', 'my country', my everything, but actually here is the cause of our discontent. The possessive 'I, me, mine and my', the manifestation of ego.

Life is just life. This life is not about you, you just make it about you, it's not personal, you just make it personal. This is a great liberating truth. Life is not about you.

No-one is trying to upset you or cause you pain, it's just how things are in this moment. No-one is trying to hurt you or destroy what you do. Your ideas and plans are not better than someone else's, but they're not worse either. Your thoughts and feelings are not less important than someone else's, but they're not more important either. When we truly know this all reasons to argue, fight and kill fall away.

We want our life to mean something, to have value and importance, but actually, it's just life. Beings are born and beings die, they all do, so relax. Surrender into the beauty and power of the Truth. Enjoy all the beautiful things that will happen for you today, and patiently be with all the others. No reason to be upset, after all, it's only life.

- 39 -
Wherever you go, there you are.

Wherever you go, there you are.

We resist and complain about our life, but do we really recognise the cause of our suffering and discontent? Of course not, and so we change many things. As much as we can in fact, sometimes going to great lengths to find happiness. We can change our car, our work, our partner, our house, even our country. We can change everything that we can think of, but until one thing changes, then each situation will work out the same way.

We carry with us the cause of our unhappiness. It goes everywhere, and is present in every moment. What is it? Why, the past of course.

This past arises in every moment, colouring what we see, hear, taste, smell and touch and then how we feel about it. Until we are able to surrender into the moment, accept what is, then respond with openness and love, we will always suffer. It does not matter where you go or what you do, until we let go of the past our life will just go round and round. This is a big, big teaching. Freedom is not about getting something, it is about releasing something.

What is that something? It is only our dedicated attachment to the past. And the way out?

See, know, understand and let go.

To let go, even a little, is the first step on your path of liberation and the first moment of real peace in your life.

- 40 -
Without our unhappiness, how could we end our unhappiness?

Without our unhappiness, how could we end our unhappiness?

As human beings our common goal is to be happy. It is our first thought in the morning and our last thought in the evening. It is what unites us all. But happiness is not something to be achieved through doing something special, or by acquiring more and more things. Happiness is the natural disposition of the mind, and so we don't have to create happiness because happiness is always there, always present and always ready to be accessed. What we need to do is let go of the causes of our unhappiness.

However, to bring about real change in our life we have to reach the point where we are truly tired of our unhappiness. But at the same time, it is important that we see unhappiness, not as the enemy, but as the condition for change. Without our unhappiness, how could we end our unhappiness?

What is it that creates these feelings within us? Once we know that we have something to work with and we can begin the process of 'letting go'. It is the letting go that makes a space for the real and lasting happiness.

So don't see your unhappiness is as the enemy, see it only as the motivation and the opportunity for beautiful change in your life.

Life is not personal

- 41 -
Be aware.

Be aware.

Take a moment and look. Look how our life spins, faster and faster each day. So many things to do, so many things to get and so little time to do it all.

Without awareness it is easy to be pulled into this madness and be completely caught up in the excitement, frustration and disappointment of life.

So be aware. Just see how things are. Don't judge. Don't formulate new opinions. Just be with things peacefully and stay in balance. Cast your web of awareness over your life and allow the space for everything to arise and pass away naturally.

Give your attention to this moment and your activity in this moment. This is your whole life, just this.

Be aware and let things be as they are.

- 42 -
It's easy to be philosophical with somebody else's life.

It's easy to be philosophical with somebody else's life.

Often we feel disconnected from the lives of others. We see people who seem to have so much good fortune and success in the material sense that we wonder how they could ever feel unhappy or complain about their lives. We fail to realise that suffering and unhappiness are aspects of mind common to all beings and that all our judgements are really only a manifestation of our own jealousies, fears and insecurites. It is always so easy to tell others just to 'let go,' of some emotional crisis whilst explaining carefully and perhaps a little patronisingly, exactly what we would do in their situation.

Without a feeling of connectedness we will always find ourselves judging and commenting on the lives of others without ever truly understanding the difficulties that they face.

Life is life, and suffering is suffering. When we understand these truths intuitively we are able to be at peace with the world and give support and service to everyone who is in need.

- 43 -

**I am not your problem,
nor am I not the solution to your problem.**

*P*ointing the finger of blame is always an easy thing to do. We meet different moments in our life which are unpleasant for us and immediately turn to the other person and say, 'It's your fault that I am unhappy', or worse, 'You did this to me!'

Not only is this not true, it never can be true! The world that we experience is always unique and personal to us. No-one can give happiness to us, nor can anyone take it away. No-one can break our heart and no-one can make us fall in love. Only we have the power to do these things. However, when we live in our sleep, we are completely unaware of our own self responsibility and so we continually give away our personal power to everyone and everything around us. We fail to see that our happiness and our unhappiness comes only from ourselves and that everything else is just imagination.

Wake up to this liberating truth, smile at each day and be free.

Life is not personal

- 44 -
Daily Loving Kindness Meditation

May I be free from anger and ill will.
May I be free from fears and anxiety.
May I be free from suffering and pain.
May I be free from ignorance and desire.
May I be happy and peaceful.
May I be harmonious.
May I be liberated from greed, hatred and delusion.
May I realise the deeper peace within.

May all beings be free from anger and ill will.
May all beings be free from fears and anxiety.
May all beings be free from all suffering and all pain.
May all beings be free from ignorance and desire.
May all beings be happy and peaceful.
May all beings be harmonious.
May all beings be liberated from greed, hatred and delusion.
May all beings realise the deeper peace within.

Empowering acceptance

Find a quiet place, relax the body, close the eyes and remind yourself to be accepting of the reality of the moment. Acceptance is always about the moment, and not longer than that.

May I accept other beings, exactly as they are in this moment.
May I accept this moment exactly as it is.
May I accept myself exactly as I am in this moment.

Michael Kewley
Dhammachariya Paññadipa

Michael Kewley, the former Buddhist monk Paññadipa, is an internationally acclaimed Dhamma Teacher and Meditation Master, conducting courses throughout Europe, India, Thailand, Israel and the U.S.A.

A disciple of the late Sayadaw Rewata Dhamma, he teaches solely on the instruction of his own Master, to share the Dhamma in the spirit of the Buddha, so that all beings might benefit.

His method of teaching is suffused with wisdom, love and humour and on his courses, seminars and intensive meditation retreats during his evening talks, Dhamma halls are filled with the sound of joyful laughter.

Michael travels extensively, but is based in the South of France.

For a full biography of Michael and videos of his teachings, visit:

www.puredhamma.org
Contact: dhammateacher@hotmail.com

Further reading from Michael Kewley:
- HIGHER THAN HAPPINESS
- OPENING THE SPIRITUAL HEART
- NOT THIS
- LIFE CHANGING MAGIC
- WALKING THE PATH
- THE OTHER SHORE
- THE REALITY OF KAMMA

www.ingramcontent.com/pod-product-compliance
Ingram Content Group UK Ltd.
Pitfield, Milton Keynes, MK11 3LW, UK
UKHW021257180426